the rainbow blueprint

an action journal

for those with

many passions

Gilat Ben-Dor

GILAT BEN-DOR MEDIA, LLC

A GUSTO POWER Book

Published by Gilat Ben-Dor Media, LLC
6501 E. Greenway Pkwy., Suite 103
PMB 519
Scottsdale, AZ 85254
USA
http://GilatMedia.com

Copyright ©2011 Gilat Ben-Dor
All rights reserved.

No part of this book may be reproduced, stored in a retrieval system, or transmitted in any language, by any means, electronic, photocopying, recording, or otherwise, without written permission from the publisher.

"The Rainbow Blueprint", "The Rainbow Blueprint Action Journal," "Multi-Passionate Professional," and "Gilat Ben-Dor Media" are trademarks of Gilat Ben-Dor and Gilat Ben-Dor Media, LLC. "Gusto Power" is a registered trademark of Gilat Ben-Dor.

Cover design and interior layout by Gilat Ben-Dor.

For information or special discounts on bulk purchases, please contact
Gilat Ben-Dor Media, LLC at address above, or email: info@GilatMedia.com

ISBN-13: 978-0-9832674-2-3
ISBN-10: 0-983267-42-1

First printed in 2011.

10 9 8 7 6 5 4 3 2 1

Printed in the U.S.A.

To all of the
passionate souls
whose dreams are
still bubbling
inside

And to my family,
my greatest
inspiration.

Additional Titles by Gilat Ben-Dor

The Confetti Path: 101 Ways to Celebrate Your Passions
and Inspire Creativity

The GUSTO POWER® Workbook: Tactics and Strategies for
the Multi-Passionate Professional™

♦♦♦♦♦

*For a complete list of Gilat Ben-Dor's publications since the last printing of
this book, please visit http://GilatMedia.com*

the rainbow blueprint

an action journal

for those with

many passions

Gilat Ben-Dor

It is never too late to be what you might have been.

-George Eliot

Contents

Introduction 1
How to Use This Journal 3
Daily Experience Pages Begin 5
Monthly Reflections: Month 1 41
Monthly Reflections: Month 2 77
Monthly Reflections: Month 3 113
Monthly Reflections: Month 4 149
Monthly Reflections: Month 5 185
Monthly Reflections: Month 6 221
Monthly Reflections: Month 7 257
Monthly Reflections: Month 8 293
Monthly Reflections: Month 9 329
Monthly Reflections: Month 10 365
Monthly Reflections: Month 11 401
Monthly Reflections: Month 12 437
Year in Review 438
About the Author 441
Rainbow Blueprint Opportunities 443

Introduction

I once took a creative writing class that required us to bring journals with us everywhere we went. Some classmates did this proudly, toting colorful diaries conspicuously under their arms, fervently jotting what came to mind at any place, any time. Others were more timid or reserved, preferring the privacy of a backpack-stashed notebook, to be fished out in decidedly solitary moments.

All we were told regarding this assignment was to "express yourself" and "write what comes to mind whenever you feel the need." Ironically, we had stringent word count requirements for our journals due each week.

In the end, was this journal experience transformative? Effective? Productive? Not for me.

Why not? There was simply no strategy behind it. There is nothing wrong with using a journal to express oneself, or to chronicle life events, or to practice one's writing; but without a strategic plan, I felt I did not need a class for this. I had already been journaling in "free form" for years, and there was nothing new with this assignment.

In theory, "journaling" is believed to be a relaxing or cathartic experience for the writer, with the potential for profound self-discovery along the way. These results can indeed hold true, but without an overarching plan or intention, we may leave these precious moments of revelation to chance. A journal with direction – not as a didactic micromanagement of what we write, but rather, one with a strategy about what we wish to accomplish with our writing— may be the most likely ticket to encountering that "aha" moment we all seek for enriching our existence.

For a journal to help accomplish one's goals, there need to be defined objectives (strategies), action steps (tactics), an execution of those action steps, and finally, periodic check points to reflect upon the effectiveness of it all.

As such, *The Rainbow Blueprint Action Journal* is not just a pretty book for jotting down random, stream-of-consciousness thoughts. Instead, *The Rainbow Blueprint Action Journal* was designed with the deliberate purpose of helping you wade through the noise (or music) of multiple passions competing and clamoring for your attention—but often, leaving you overwhelmed and back where you started.

The question is, are you committed? Do you *want* to consciously move through your days taking the necessary steps to incorporate your passions in a big way? This is no idle process. This is a process that rewards consistency, determination, and the courage to reflect without distraction. If you are up for this richly rewarding challenge, be prepared to be transformed: go from *talking* about your passions to doing them; go from *dreaming* about your passions to figuring out that ideal mix of activities and focus that will transform your days into a more peaceful yet purposeful journey, knowing that you are touching upon all of your key passions in a given day, week, or month.

Most likely, if you naturally have many passions then you have also been gifted with the energy, curiosity, and drive to earnestly attempt the pursuit of all (or most) of them. Now it becomes a matter of staying on track. The goal of *The Rainbow Blueprint Action Journal* is to offer you the space, physically and mentally, emotionally and spiritually, to plan, execute, and reflect specifically on this purpose: on the way you currently approach your days in the context of your passions, with check points built in to keep you accountable to your own intentions.

The Rainbow Blueprint Action Journal is not an appointment book, a schedule ledger, or an errand tracker. Instead, it is a private place for you to centralize your thoughts, formulate a vision, and—most importantly—follow these with action, to achieve a fulfilling life through a rainbow of passions.

Gilat Ben-Dor
Scottsdale, Arizona

How to Use This Journal

The Rainbow Blueprint Action Journal encompasses one year of activity, left undated so that you can begin at any time. The journal is comprised of four parts: the **Daily Experience Pages**, the **Weekly Summary**, the **Monthly Reflections**, and the **Year in Review**. All pages have been left unlined for added freedom.

The **Daily Experience Pages**, which make up the majority of this journal, can be completed as a planning tool for the day ahead, as a review of the how the day went, or as both. The Morning Intention statement encourages you to think about your areas of focus for the coming day, and to later gauge how the day went in accordance with your intention.

The **Weekly Summary** is an opportunity to look back at the past week and see if you are heading in the direction that feels right. By checking in with yourself on a weekly basis, you offer yourself an "early warning system" in case you have been sidetracked away from your own intentions for the week.

You will find **Monthly Reflections** at the end of each month. Just as the Weekly Summary can be used to stay the course, the Monthly Reflections reveal deeper trends (and their outcomes) as you continue your journey of planning and practice. The Monthly Reflections are also a good time to check in with yourself, and ensure that your chosen plan is still relevant to your ever-evolving state of being. The idea is not to feel obligated to continue with goals you no longer enjoy, but keep yourself current: take time at the end of each month to revisit your goals and passions, and ensure that they are still aligned.

At the end of the year, congratulate yourself! Look back on the year, re-read your journal entries, and study your Monthly Reflections. See how far you've come, the progress you've made, and the growth you have experienced. Then, set aside a quiet session to evaluate your progress and complete the **Year in Review** collection of questions. I encourage you to think not only of the year that has passed, but to look ahead to the coming year and its new goals and intentions.

Remember, as you complete each page of the journal, no two days will likely be the same and yet patterns and habits may emerge from the timeframes you capture. That is an essential part of the road to discovery, as you accumulate pages of raw experiences and documented reflections. There is certainly no "right" or "wrong" way to go about using the journal. With consistent use, you will see that it is possible to have many passions without feeling scattered or torn.

The Rainbow Blueprint Action Journal is a versatile tool to help corral your interests, talents and visions into a richly varied, yet cohesive lifestyle *based on your thoughts, planning, action and reflection.* As you practice deliberate planning around your passions, you will foster personal growth, sharpen your focus, and finally feel organized as you successfully live a life of multiple passions.

Daily Experience Pages

Date_____

Morning Intention: *Today will be all about...*

Today's Triumphs:

Today's Challenges:

Which of my passions did I touch upon today?

Was this combination of passions successful for me? Why or why not?

Date_____

Morning Intention: *Today will be all about...*

Today's Triumphs:

Today's Challenges:

Which of my passions did I touch upon today?

Was this combination of passions successful for me? Why or why not?

Daily Experience Pages

Date_____

Morning Intention: *Today will be all about...*

Today's Triumphs:

Today's Challenges:

Which of my passions did I touch upon today?

Was this combination of passions successful for me? Why or why not?

Date_____

Morning Intention: *Today will be all about...*

Today's Triumphs:

Today's Challenges:

Which of my passions did I touch upon today?

Was this combination of passions successful for me? Why or why not?

Date_____

Morning Intention: *Today will be all about...*

Today's Triumphs:

Today's Challenges:

Which of my passions did I touch upon today?

Was this combination of passions successful for me? Why or why not?

Date_____

Morning Intention: *Today will be all about...*

Today's Triumphs:

Today's Challenges:

Which of my passions did I touch upon today?

Was this combination of passions successful for me? Why or why not?

Daily Experience Pages

Date_____

Morning Intention: *Today will be all about...*

Today's Triumphs:

Today's Challenges:

Which of my passions did I touch upon today?

Was this combination of passions successful for me? Why or why not?

Weekly Summary

What were my top three areas of focus this week?

What should I continue to focus on in the coming week?

What will be a new area of focus to add to, or change, from the past week?

What were my top three challenges this week?

How can I improve on each challenge moving forward?

Daily Experience Pages

Date_____

Morning Intention: *Today will be all about...*

Today's Triumphs:

Today's Challenges:

Which of my passions did I touch upon today?

Was this combination of passions successful for me? Why or why not?

Date_____

Morning Intention: *Today will be all about...*

Today's Triumphs:

Today's Challenges:

Which of my passions did I touch upon today?

Was this combination of passions successful for me? Why or why not?

Date_____

Morning Intention: *Today will be all about...*

Today's Triumphs:

Today's Challenges:

Which of my passions did I touch upon today?

Was this combination of passions successful for me? Why or why not?

Date_____

Morning Intention: *Today will be all about...*

Today's Triumphs:

Today's Challenges:

Which of my passions did I touch upon today?

Was this combination of passions successful for me? Why or why not?

Date_____

Morning Intention: *Today will be all about...*

Today's Triumphs:

Today's Challenges:

Which of my passions did I touch upon today?

Was this combination of passions successful for me? Why or why not?

Date_____

Morning Intention: *Today will be all about...*

Today's Triumphs:

Today's Challenges:

Which of my passions did I touch upon today?

Was this combination of passions successful for me? Why or why not?

Date_____

Morning Intention: *Today will be all about...*

Today's Triumphs:

Today's Challenges:

Which of my passions did I touch upon today?

Was this combination of passions successful for me? Why or why not?

Weekly Summary

What were my top three areas of focus this week?

What should I continue to focus on in the coming week?

What will be a new area of focus to add to, or change, from the past week?

What were my top three challenges this week?

How can I improve on each challenge moving forward?

Daily Experience Pages

Date_____

Morning Intention: *Today will be all about...*

Today's Triumphs:

Today's Challenges:

Which of my passions did I touch upon today?

Was this combination of passions successful for me? Why or why not?

Daily Experience Pages 23

Date_____

Morning Intention: *Today will be all about...*

Today's Triumphs:

Today's Challenges:

Which of my passions did I touch upon today?

Was this combination of passions successful for me? Why or why not?

Date_____

Morning Intention: *Today will be all about...*

Today's Triumphs:

Today's Challenges:

Which of my passions did I touch upon today?

Was this combination of passions successful for me? Why or why not?

Date_____

Morning Intention: *Today will be all about...*

Today's Triumphs:

Today's Challenges:

Which of my passions did I touch upon today?

Was this combination of passions successful for me? Why or why not?

Date_____

Morning Intention: *Today will be all about...*

Today's Triumphs:

Today's Challenges:

Which of my passions did I touch upon today?

Was this combination of passions successful for me? Why or why not?

Date_____

Morning Intention: *Today will be all about...*

Today's Triumphs:

Today's Challenges:

Which of my passions did I touch upon today?

Was this combination of passions successful for me? Why or why not?

Date_____

Morning Intention: *Today will be all about...*

Today's Triumphs:

Today's Challenges:

Which of my passions did I touch upon today?

Was this combination of passions successful for me? Why or why not?

Weekly Summary

What were my top three areas of focus this week?

What should I continue to focus on in the coming week?

What will be a new area of focus to add to, or change, from the past week?

What were my top three challenges this week?

How can I improve on each challenge moving forward?

Daily Experience Pages

Date_____

Morning Intention: *Today will be all about...*

Today's Triumphs:

Today's Challenges:

Which of my passions did I touch upon today?

Was this combination of passions successful for me? Why or why not?

Daily Experience Pages 31

Date_____

Morning Intention: *Today will be all about...*

Today's Triumphs:

Today's Challenges:

Which of my passions did I touch upon today?

Was this combination of passions successful for me? Why or why not?

Date_____

Morning Intention: *Today will be all about...*

Today's Triumphs:

Today's Challenges:

Which of my passions did I touch upon today?

Was this combination of passions successful for me? Why or why not?

Date_____

Morning Intention: *Today will be all about...*

Today's Triumphs:

Today's Challenges:

Which of my passions did I touch upon today?

Was this combination of passions successful for me? Why or why not?

Date_____

Morning Intention: *Today will be all about...*

Today's Triumphs:

Today's Challenges:

Which of my passions did I touch upon today?

Was this combination of passions successful for me? Why or why not?

Date_____

Morning Intention: *Today will be all about...*

Today's Triumphs:

Today's Challenges:

Which of my passions did I touch upon today?

Was this combination of passions successful for me? Why or why not?

Date_____

Morning Intention: *Today will be all about...*

Today's Triumphs:

Today's Challenges:

Which of my passions did I touch upon today?

Was this combination of passions successful for me? Why or why not?

Weekly Summary

What were my top three areas of focus this week?

What should I continue to focus on in the coming week?

What will be a new area of focus to add to, or change, from the past week?

What were my top three challenges this week?

How can I improve on each challenge moving forward?

Date_____

Morning Intention: *Today will be all about...*

Today's Triumphs:

Today's Challenges:

Which of my passions did I touch upon today?

Was this combination of passions successful for me? Why or why not?

Date_____

Morning Intention: *Today will be all about...*

Today's Triumphs:

Today's Challenges:

Which of my passions did I touch upon today?

Was this combination of passions successful for me? Why or why not?

Date_____

Morning Intention: *Today will be all about...*

Today's Triumphs:

Today's Challenges:

Which of my passions did I touch upon today?

Was this combination of passions successful for me? Why or why not?

Monthly Reflections: Month 1

If I continue along my current path, is it likely I will incorporate all of my key passions into my life in the coming month?

The next 3 months?

The next 6 months?

By the end of the year?

Patterns or trends I have noticed this past month:

Positive:

Negative:

In the coming month, I plan to continue to:

In the coming month, I plan to avoid or reduce:

Daily Experience Pages

Date_____

Morning Intention: *Today will be all about...*

Today's Triumphs:

Today's Challenges:

Which of my passions did I touch upon today?

Was this combination of passions successful for me? Why or why not?

Date_____

Morning Intention: *Today will be all about...*

Today's Triumphs:

Today's Challenges:

Which of my passions did I touch upon today?

Was this combination of passions successful for me? Why or why not?

Date_____

Morning Intention: *Today will be all about...*

Today's Triumphs:

Today's Challenges:

Which of my passions did I touch upon today?

Was this combination of passions successful for me? Why or why not?

Date_____

Morning Intention: *Today will be all about...*

Today's Triumphs:

Today's Challenges:

Which of my passions did I touch upon today?

Was this combination of passions successful for me? Why or why not?

Date_____

Morning Intention: *Today will be all about...*

Today's Triumphs:

Today's Challenges:

Which of my passions did I touch upon today?

Was this combination of passions successful for me? Why or why not?

Date _____

Morning Intention: *Today will be all about...*

Today's Triumphs:

Today's Challenges:

Which of my passions did I touch upon today?

Was this combination of passions successful for me? Why or why not?

Date_____

Morning Intention: *Today will be all about...*

Today's Triumphs:

Today's Challenges:

Which of my passions did I touch upon today?

Was this combination of passions successful for me? Why or why not?

Weekly Summary

What were my top three areas of focus this week?

What should I continue to focus on in the coming week?

What will be a new area of focus to add to, or change, from the past week?

What were my top three challenges this week?

How can I improve on each challenge moving forward?

Daily Experience Pages

Date_____

Morning Intention: *Today will be all about...*

Today's Triumphs:

Today's Challenges:

Which of my passions did I touch upon today?

Was this combination of passions successful for me? Why or why not?

Date_____

Morning Intention: *Today will be all about...*

Today's Triumphs:

Today's Challenges:

Which of my passions did I touch upon today?

Was this combination of passions successful for me? Why or why not?

Date_____

Morning Intention: *Today will be all about...*

Today's Triumphs:

Today's Challenges:

Which of my passions did I touch upon today?

Was this combination of passions successful for me? Why or why not?

Date_____

Morning Intention: *Today will be all about...*

Today's Triumphs:

Today's Challenges:

Which of my passions did I touch upon today?

Was this combination of passions successful for me? Why or why not?

Date_____

Morning Intention: *Today will be all about...*

Today's Triumphs:

Today's Challenges:

Which of my passions did I touch upon today?

Was this combination of passions successful for me? Why or why not?

Date_____

Morning Intention: *Today will be all about...*

Today's Triumphs:

Today's Challenges:

Which of my passions did I touch upon today?

Was this combination of passions successful for me? Why or why not?

Date_____

Morning Intention: *Today will be all about...*

Today's Triumphs:

Today's Challenges:

Which of my passions did I touch upon today?

Was this combination of passions successful for me? Why or why not?

Weekly Summary

What were my top three areas of focus this week?

What should I continue to focus on in the coming week?

What will be a new area of focus to add to, or change, from the past week?

What were my top three challenges this week?

How can I improve on each challenge moving forward?

Daily Experience Pages

Date_____

Morning Intention: *Today will be all about...*

Today's Triumphs:

Today's Challenges:

Which of my passions did I touch upon today?

Was this combination of passions successful for me? Why or why not?

Date_____

Morning Intention: *Today will be all about...*

Today's Triumphs:

Today's Challenges:

Which of my passions did I touch upon today?

Was this combination of passions successful for me? Why or why not?

Date_____

Morning Intention: *Today will be all about...*

Today's Triumphs:

Today's Challenges:

Which of my passions did I touch upon today?

Was this combination of passions successful for me? Why or why not?

Date_____

Morning Intention: *Today will be all about...*

Today's Triumphs:

Today's Challenges:

Which of my passions did I touch upon today?

Was this combination of passions successful for me? Why or why not?

Date_____

Morning Intention: *Today will be all about...*

Today's Triumphs:

Today's Challenges:

Which of my passions did I touch upon today?

Was this combination of passions successful for me? Why or why not?

Date_____

Morning Intention: *Today will be all about...*

Today's Triumphs:

Today's Challenges:

Which of my passions did I touch upon today?

Was this combination of passions successful for me? Why or why not?

Date_____

Morning Intention: *Today will be all about...*

Today's Triumphs:

Today's Challenges:

Which of my passions did I touch upon today?

Was this combination of passions successful for me? Why or why not?

Weekly Summary

What were my top three areas of focus this week?

What should I continue to focus on in the coming week?

What will be a new area of focus to add to, or change, from the past week?

What were my top three challenges this week?

How can I improve on each challenge moving forward?

Daily Experience Pages

Date_____

Morning Intention: *Today will be all about...*

Today's Triumphs:

Today's Challenges:

Which of my passions did I touch upon today?

Was this combination of passions successful for me? Why or why not?

Date_____

Morning Intention: *Today will be all about...*

Today's Triumphs:

Today's Challenges:

Which of my passions did I touch upon today?

Was this combination of passions successful for me? Why or why not?

Date_____

Morning Intention: *Today will be all about...*

Today's Triumphs:

Today's Challenges:

Which of my passions did I touch upon today?

Was this combination of passions successful for me? Why or why not?

Daily Experience Pages

Date_____

Morning Intention: *Today will be all about...*

Today's Triumphs:

Today's Challenges:

Which of my passions did I touch upon today?

Was this combination of passions successful for me? Why or why not?

Date_____

Morning Intention: *Today will be all about...*

Today's Triumphs:

Today's Challenges:

Which of my passions did I touch upon today?

Was this combination of passions successful for me? Why or why not?

Date_____

Morning Intention: *Today will be all about...*

Today's Triumphs:

Today's Challenges:

Which of my passions did I touch upon today?

Was this combination of passions successful for me? Why or why not?

Date_____

Morning Intention: *Today will be all about...*

Today's Triumphs:

Today's Challenges:

Which of my passions did I touch upon today?

Was this combination of passions successful for me? Why or why not?

Weekly Summary

What were my top three areas of focus this week?

What should I continue to focus on in the coming week?

What will be a new area of focus to add to, or change, from the past week?

What were my top three challenges this week?

How can I improve on each challenge moving forward?

Date_____

Morning Intention: *Today will be all about...*

Today's Triumphs:

Today's Challenges:

Which of my passions did I touch upon today?

Was this combination of passions successful for me? Why or why not?

Date_____

Morning Intention: *Today will be all about...*

Today's Triumphs:

Today's Challenges:

Which of my passions did I touch upon today?

Was this combination of passions successful for me? Why or why not?

Date_____

Morning Intention: *Today will be all about...*

Today's Triumphs:

Today's Challenges:

Which of my passions did I touch upon today?

Was this combination of passions successful for me? Why or why not?

Monthly Reflections: Month 2

If I continue along my current path, is it likely I will incorporate all of my key passions into my life in the coming month?

The next 3 months?

The next 6 months?

By the end of the year?

Patterns or trends I have noticed this past month:

Positive:

Negative:

In the coming month, I plan to continue to:

In the coming month, I plan to avoid or reduce:

Daily Experience Pages

Date_____

Morning Intention: *Today will be all about...*

Today's Triumphs:

Today's Challenges:

Which of my passions did I touch upon today?

Was this combination of passions successful for me? Why or why not?

Date_____

Morning Intention: *Today will be all about...*

Today's Triumphs:

Today's Challenges:

Which of my passions did I touch upon today?

Was this combination of passions successful for me? Why or why not?

Date_____

Morning Intention: *Today will be all about...*

Today's Triumphs:

Today's Challenges:

Which of my passions did I touch upon today?

Was this combination of passions successful for me? Why or why not?

Date_____

Morning Intention: *Today will be all about...*

Today's Triumphs:

Today's Challenges:

Which of my passions did I touch upon today?

Was this combination of passions successful for me? Why or why not?

Date_____

Morning Intention: *Today will be all about...*

Today's Triumphs:

Today's Challenges:

Which of my passions did I touch upon today?

Was this combination of passions successful for me? Why or why not?

Date_____

Morning Intention: *Today will be all about...*

Today's Triumphs:

Today's Challenges:

Which of my passions did I touch upon today?

Was this combination of passions successful for me? Why or why not?

Date_____

Morning Intention: *Today will be all about...*

Today's Triumphs:

Today's Challenges:

Which of my passions did I touch upon today?

Was this combination of passions successful for me? Why or why not?

Weekly Summary

What were my top three areas of focus this week?

What should I continue to focus on in the coming week?

What will be a new area of focus to add to, or change, from the past week?

What were my top three challenges this week?

How can I improve on each challenge moving forward?

Daily Experience Pages

Date_____

Morning Intention: *Today will be all about...*

Today's Triumphs:

Today's Challenges:

Which of my passions did I touch upon today?

Was this combination of passions successful for me? Why or why not?

Date_____

Morning Intention: *Today will be all about...*

Today's Triumphs:

Today's Challenges:

Which of my passions did I touch upon today?

Was this combination of passions successful for me? Why or why not?

Date_____

Morning Intention: *Today will be all about...*

Today's Triumphs:

Today's Challenges:

Which of my passions did I touch upon today?

Was this combination of passions successful for me? Why or why not?

Date_____

Morning Intention: *Today will be all about...*

Today's Triumphs:

Today's Challenges:

Which of my passions did I touch upon today?

Was this combination of passions successful for me? Why or why not?

Date_____

Morning Intention: *Today will be all about...*

Today's Triumphs:

Today's Challenges:

Which of my passions did I touch upon today?

Was this combination of passions successful for me? Why or why not?

Date_____

Morning Intention: *Today will be all about...*

Today's Triumphs:

Today's Challenges:

Which of my passions did I touch upon today?

Was this combination of passions successful for me? Why or why not?

Date_____

Morning Intention: *Today will be all about...*

Today's Triumphs:

Today's Challenges:

Which of my passions did I touch upon today?

Was this combination of passions successful for me? Why or why not?

Weekly Summary

What were my top three areas of focus this week?

What should I continue to focus on in the coming week?

What will be a new area of focus to add to, or change, from the past week?

What were my top three challenges this week?

How can I improve on each challenge moving forward?

Daily Experience Pages

Date_____

Morning Intention: *Today will be all about...*

Today's Triumphs:

Today's Challenges:

Which of my passions did I touch upon today?

Was this combination of passions successful for me? Why or why not?

Date_____

Morning Intention: *Today will be all about...*

Today's Triumphs:

Today's Challenges:

Which of my passions did I touch upon today?

Was this combination of passions successful for me? Why or why not?

Date_____

Morning Intention: *Today will be all about...*

Today's Triumphs:

Today's Challenges:

Which of my passions did I touch upon today?

Was this combination of passions successful for me? Why or why not?

Daily Experience Pages

Date_____

Morning Intention: *Today will be all about...*

Today's Triumphs:

Today's Challenges:

Which of my passions did I touch upon today?

Was this combination of passions successful for me? Why or why not?

Date_____

Morning Intention: *Today will be all about...*

Today's Triumphs:

Today's Challenges:

Which of my passions did I touch upon today?

Was this combination of passions successful for me? Why or why not?

Daily Experience Pages

Date_____

Morning Intention: *Today will be all about...*

Today's Triumphs:

Today's Challenges:

Which of my passions did I touch upon today?

Was this combination of passions successful for me? Why or why not?

Date_____

Morning Intention: *Today will be all about...*

Today's Triumphs:

Today's Challenges:

Which of my passions did I touch upon today?

Was this combination of passions successful for me? Why or why not?

Weekly Summary

What were my top three areas of focus this week?

What should I continue to focus on in the coming week?

What will be a new area of focus to add to, or change, from the past week?

What were my top three challenges this week?

How can I improve on each challenge moving forward?

Daily Experience Pages

Date_____

Morning Intention: *Today will be all about...*

Today's Triumphs:

Today's Challenges:

Which of my passions did I touch upon today?

Was this combination of passions successful for me? Why or why not?

Date_____

Morning Intention: *Today will be all about...*

Today's Triumphs:

Today's Challenges:

Which of my passions did I touch upon today?

Was this combination of passions successful for me? Why or why not?

Date_____

Morning Intention: *Today will be all about...*

Today's Triumphs:

Today's Challenges:

Which of my passions did I touch upon today?

Was this combination of passions successful for me? Why or why not?

Date_____

Morning Intention: *Today will be all about...*

Today's Triumphs:

Today's Challenges:

Which of my passions did I touch upon today?

Was this combination of passions successful for me? Why or why not?

Date_____

Morning Intention: *Today will be all about...*

Today's Triumphs:

Today's Challenges:

Which of my passions did I touch upon today?

Was this combination of passions successful for me? Why or why not?

Date_____

Morning Intention: *Today will be all about...*

Today's Triumphs:

Today's Challenges:

Which of my passions did I touch upon today?

Was this combination of passions successful for me? Why or why not?

Date_____

Morning Intention: *Today will be all about...*

Today's Triumphs:

Today's Challenges:

Which of my passions did I touch upon today?

Was this combination of passions successful for me? Why or why not?

Weekly Summary

What were my top three areas of focus this week?

What should I continue to focus on in the coming week?

What will be a new area of focus to add to, or change, from the past week?

What were my top three challenges this week?

How can I improve on each challenge moving forward?

Date_____

Morning Intention: *Today will be all about...*

Today's Triumphs:

Today's Challenges:

Which of my passions did I touch upon today?

Was this combination of passions successful for me? Why or why not?

Date_____

Morning Intention: *Today will be all about...*

Today's Triumphs:

Today's Challenges:

Which of my passions did I touch upon today?

Was this combination of passions successful for me? Why or why not?

Date_____

Morning Intention: *Today will be all about...*

Today's Triumphs:

Today's Challenges:

Which of my passions did I touch upon today?

Was this combination of passions successful for me? Why or why not?

Monthly Reflections: Month 3

If I continue along my current path, is it likely I will incorporate all of my key passions into my life in the coming month?

The next 3 months?

The next 6 months?

By the end of the year?

Patterns or trends I have noticed this past month:

Positive:

Negative:

In the coming month, I plan to continue to:

In the coming month, I plan to avoid or reduce:

Daily Experience Pages

Date_____

Morning Intention: *Today will be all about...*

Today's Triumphs:

Today's Challenges:

Which of my passions did I touch upon today?

Was this combination of passions successful for me? Why or why not?

Date_____

Morning Intention: *Today will be all about...*

Today's Triumphs:

Today's Challenges:

Which of my passions did I touch upon today?

Was this combination of passions successful for me? Why or why not?

Date_____

Morning Intention: *Today will be all about…*

Today's Triumphs:

Today's Challenges:

Which of my passions did I touch upon today?

Was this combination of passions successful for me? Why or why not?

Date_____

Morning Intention: *Today will be all about...*

Today's Triumphs:

Today's Challenges:

Which of my passions did I touch upon today?

Was this combination of passions successful for me? Why or why not?

Date_____

Morning Intention: *Today will be all about...*

Today's Triumphs:

Today's Challenges:

Which of my passions did I touch upon today?

Was this combination of passions successful for me? Why or why not?

Date_____

Morning Intention: *Today will be all about...*

Today's Triumphs:

Today's Challenges:

Which of my passions did I touch upon today?

Was this combination of passions successful for me? Why or why not?

Date_____

Morning Intention: *Today will be all about...*

Today's Triumphs:

Today's Challenges:

Which of my passions did I touch upon today?

Was this combination of passions successful for me? Why or why not?

Weekly Summary

What were my top three areas of focus this week?

What should I continue to focus on in the coming week?

What will be a new area of focus to add to, or change, from the past week?

What were my top three challenges this week?

How can I improve on each challenge moving forward?

Daily Experience Pages

Date_____

Morning Intention: *Today will be all about...*

Today's Triumphs:

Today's Challenges:

Which of my passions did I touch upon today?

Was this combination of passions successful for me? Why or why not?

Date_____

Morning Intention: *Today will be all about...*

Today's Triumphs:

Today's Challenges:

Which of my passions did I touch upon today?

Was this combination of passions successful for me? Why or why not?

Date_____

Morning Intention: *Today will be all about…*

Today's Triumphs:

Today's Challenges:

Which of my passions did I touch upon today?

Was this combination of passions successful for me? Why or why not?

Date_____

Morning Intention: *Today will be all about...*

Today's Triumphs:

Today's Challenges:

Which of my passions did I touch upon today?

Was this combination of passions successful for me? Why or why not?

Date_____

Morning Intention: *Today will be all about...*

Today's Triumphs:

Today's Challenges:

Which of my passions did I touch upon today?

Was this combination of passions successful for me? Why or why not?

Date_____

Morning Intention: *Today will be all about...*

Today's Triumphs:

Today's Challenges:

Which of my passions did I touch upon today?

Was this combination of passions successful for me? Why or why not?

Date_____

Morning Intention: *Today will be all about...*

Today's Triumphs:

Today's Challenges:

Which of my passions did I touch upon today?

Was this combination of passions successful for me? Why or why not?

Weekly Summary

What were my top three areas of focus this week?

What should I continue to focus on in the coming week?

What will be a new area of focus to add to, or change, from the past week?

What were my top three challenges this week?

How can I improve on each challenge moving forward?

Daily Experience Pages

Date_____

Morning Intention: *Today will be all about...*

Today's Triumphs:

Today's Challenges:

Which of my passions did I touch upon today?

Was this combination of passions successful for me? Why or why not?

Date_____

Morning Intention: *Today will be all about...*

Today's Triumphs:

Today's Challenges:

Which of my passions did I touch upon today?

Was this combination of passions successful for me? Why or why not?

Date_____

Morning Intention: *Today will be all about...*

Today's Triumphs:

Today's Challenges:

Which of my passions did I touch upon today?

Was this combination of passions successful for me? Why or why not?

Date_____

Morning Intention: *Today will be all about...*

Today's Triumphs:

Today's Challenges:

Which of my passions did I touch upon today?

Was this combination of passions successful for me? Why or why not?

Date_____

Morning Intention: *Today will be all about...*

Today's Triumphs:

Today's Challenges:

Which of my passions did I touch upon today?

Was this combination of passions successful for me? Why or why not?

Date_____

Morning Intention: *Today will be all about...*

Today's Triumphs:

Today's Challenges:

Which of my passions did I touch upon today?

Was this combination of passions successful for me? Why or why not?

Date_____

Morning Intention: *Today will be all about...*

Today's Triumphs:

Today's Challenges:

Which of my passions did I touch upon today?

Was this combination of passions successful for me? Why or why not?

Weekly Summary

What were my top three areas of focus this week?

What should I continue to focus on in the coming week?

What will be a new area of focus to add to, or change, from the past week?

What were my top three challenges this week?

How can I improve on each challenge moving forward?

Daily Experience Pages

Date_____

Morning Intention: *Today will be all about...*

Today's Triumphs:

Today's Challenges:

Which of my passions did I touch upon today?

Was this combination of passions successful for me? Why or why not?

Date_____

Morning Intention: *Today will be all about...*

Today's Triumphs:

Today's Challenges:

Which of my passions did I touch upon today?

Was this combination of passions successful for me? Why or why not?

Date_____

Morning Intention: *Today will be all about...*

Today's Triumphs:

Today's Challenges:

Which of my passions did I touch upon today?

Was this combination of passions successful for me? Why or why not?

Date_____

Morning Intention: *Today will be all about…*

Today's Triumphs:

Today's Challenges:

Which of my passions did I touch upon today?

Was this combination of passions successful for me? Why or why not?

Date_____

Morning Intention: *Today will be all about...*

Today's Triumphs:

Today's Challenges:

Which of my passions did I touch upon today?

Was this combination of passions successful for me? Why or why not?

Date_____

Morning Intention: *Today will be all about...*

Today's Triumphs:

Today's Challenges:

Which of my passions did I touch upon today?

Was this combination of passions successful for me? Why or why not?

Date_____

Morning Intention: *Today will be all about...*

Today's Triumphs:

Today's Challenges:

Which of my passions did I touch upon today?

Was this combination of passions successful for me? Why or why not?

Weekly Summary

What were my top three areas of focus this week?

What should I continue to focus on in the coming week?

What will be a new area of focus to add to, or change, from the past week?

What were my top three challenges this week?

How can I improve on each challenge moving forward?

Date_____

Morning Intention: *Today will be all about...*

Today's Triumphs:

Today's Challenges:

Which of my passions did I touch upon today?

Was this combination of passions successful for me? Why or why not?

Date_____

Morning Intention: *Today will be all about...*

Today's Triumphs:

Today's Challenges:

Which of my passions did I touch upon today?

Was this combination of passions successful for me? Why or why not?

Date_____

Morning Intention: *Today will be all about...*

Today's Triumphs:

Today's Challenges:

Which of my passions did I touch upon today?

Was this combination of passions successful for me? Why or why not?

Monthly Reflections: Month 4

If I continue along my current path, is it likely I will incorporate all of my key passions into my life in the coming month?

The next 3 months?

The next 6 months?

By the end of the year?

Patterns or trends I have noticed this past month:

Positive:

Negative:

In the coming month, I plan to continue to:

In the coming month, I plan to avoid or reduce:

Daily Experience Pages

Date_____

Morning Intention: *Today will be all about...*

Today's Triumphs:

Today's Challenges:

Which of my passions did I touch upon today?

Was this combination of passions successful for me? Why or why not?

Date_____

Morning Intention: *Today will be all about...*

Today's Triumphs:

Today's Challenges:

Which of my passions did I touch upon today?

Was this combination of passions successful for me? Why or why not?

Date_____

Morning Intention: *Today will be all about...*

Today's Triumphs:

Today's Challenges:

Which of my passions did I touch upon today?

Was this combination of passions successful for me? Why or why not?

Date_____

Morning Intention: *Today will be all about...*

Today's Triumphs:

Today's Challenges:

Which of my passions did I touch upon today?

Was this combination of passions successful for me? Why or why not?

Date_____

Morning Intention: *Today will be all about...*

Today's Triumphs:

Today's Challenges:

Which of my passions did I touch upon today?

Was this combination of passions successful for me? Why or why not?

Date_____

Morning Intention: *Today will be all about...*

Today's Triumphs:

Today's Challenges:

Which of my passions did I touch upon today?

Was this combination of passions successful for me? Why or why not?

Date_____

Morning Intention: *Today will be all about...*

Today's Triumphs:

Today's Challenges:

Which of my passions did I touch upon today?

Was this combination of passions successful for me? Why or why not?

Weekly Summary

What were my top three areas of focus this week?

What should I continue to focus on in the coming week?

What will be a new area of focus to add to, or change, from the past week?

What were my top three challenges this week?

How can I improve on each challenge moving forward?

Daily Experience Pages

Date_____

Morning Intention: *Today will be all about...*

Today's Triumphs:

Today's Challenges:

Which of my passions did I touch upon today?

Was this combination of passions successful for me? Why or why not?

Date_____

Morning Intention: *Today will be all about...*

Today's Triumphs:

Today's Challenges:

Which of my passions did I touch upon today?

Was this combination of passions successful for me? Why or why not?

Date_____

Morning Intention: *Today will be all about...*

Today's Triumphs:

Today's Challenges:

Which of my passions did I touch upon today?

Was this combination of passions successful for me? Why or why not?

Date_____

Morning Intention: *Today will be all about...*

Today's Triumphs:

Today's Challenges:

Which of my passions did I touch upon today?

Was this combination of passions successful for me? Why or why not?

Date_____

Morning Intention: *Today will be all about...*

Today's Triumphs:

Today's Challenges:

Which of my passions did I touch upon today?

Was this combination of passions successful for me? Why or why not?

Date_____

Morning Intention: *Today will be all about...*

Today's Triumphs:

Today's Challenges:

Which of my passions did I touch upon today?

Was this combination of passions successful for me? Why or why not?

Date_____

Morning Intention: *Today will be all about...*

Today's Triumphs:

Today's Challenges:

Which of my passions did I touch upon today?

Was this combination of passions successful for me? Why or why not?

Weekly Summary

What were my top three areas of focus this week?

What should I continue to focus on in the coming week?

What will be a new area of focus to add to, or change, from the past week?

What were my top three challenges this week?

How can I improve on each challenge moving forward?

Daily Experience Pages

Date_____

Morning Intention: *Today will be all about...*

Today's Triumphs:

Today's Challenges:

Which of my passions did I touch upon today?

Was this combination of passions successful for me? Why or why not?

Date_____

Morning Intention: *Today will be all about...*

Today's Triumphs:

Today's Challenges:

Which of my passions did I touch upon today?

Was this combination of passions successful for me? Why or why not?

Date_____

Morning Intention: *Today will be all about...*

Today's Triumphs:

Today's Challenges:

Which of my passions did I touch upon today?

Was this combination of passions successful for me? Why or why not?

Date_____

Morning Intention: *Today will be all about...*

Today's Triumphs:

Today's Challenges:

Which of my passions did I touch upon today?

Was this combination of passions successful for me? Why or why not?

Date_____

Morning Intention: *Today will be all about...*

Today's Triumphs:

Today's Challenges:

Which of my passions did I touch upon today?

Was this combination of passions successful for me? Why or why not?

Date_____

Morning Intention: *Today will be all about...*

Today's Triumphs:

Today's Challenges:

Which of my passions did I touch upon today?

Was this combination of passions successful for me? Why or why not?

Date_____

Morning Intention: *Today will be all about...*

Today's Triumphs:

Today's Challenges:

Which of my passions did I touch upon today?

Was this combination of passions successful for me? Why or why not?

Weekly Summary

What were my top three areas of focus this week?

What should I continue to focus on in the coming week?

What will be a new area of focus to add to, or change, from the past week?

What were my top three challenges this week?

How can I improve on each challenge moving forward?

Daily Experience Pages

Date_____

Morning Intention: *Today will be all about...*

Today's Triumphs:

Today's Challenges:

Which of my passions did I touch upon today?

Was this combination of passions successful for me? Why or why not?

Date_____

Morning Intention: *Today will be all about...*

Today's Triumphs:

Today's Challenges:

Which of my passions did I touch upon today?

Was this combination of passions successful for me? Why or why not?

Date_____

Morning Intention: *Today will be all about...*

Today's Triumphs:

Today's Challenges:

Which of my passions did I touch upon today?

Was this combination of passions successful for me? Why or why not?

Date_____

Morning Intention: *Today will be all about...*

Today's Triumphs:

Today's Challenges:

Which of my passions did I touch upon today?

Was this combination of passions successful for me? Why or why not?

Date_____

Morning Intention: *Today will be all about...*

Today's Triumphs:

Today's Challenges:

Which of my passions did I touch upon today?

Was this combination of passions successful for me? Why or why not?

Date_____

Morning Intention: *Today will be all about...*

Today's Triumphs:

Today's Challenges:

Which of my passions did I touch upon today?

Was this combination of passions successful for me? Why or why not?

Date_____

Morning Intention: *Today will be all about...*

Today's Triumphs:

Today's Challenges:

Which of my passions did I touch upon today?

Was this combination of passions successful for me? Why or why not?

Weekly Summary

What were my top three areas of focus this week?

What should I continue to focus on in the coming week?

What will be a new area of focus to add to, or change, from the past week?

What were my top three challenges this week?

How can I improve on each challenge moving forward?

Date_____

Morning Intention: *Today will be all about...*

Today's Triumphs:

Today's Challenges:

Which of my passions did I touch upon today?

Was this combination of passions successful for me? Why or why not?

Date_____

Morning Intention: *Today will be all about...*

Today's Triumphs:

Today's Challenges:

Which of my passions did I touch upon today?

Was this combination of passions successful for me? Why or why not?

Date_____

Morning Intention: *Today will be all about...*

Today's Triumphs:

Today's Challenges:

Which of my passions did I touch upon today?

Was this combination of passions successful for me? Why or why not?

Monthly Reflections: Month 5

If I continue along my current path, is it likely I will incorporate all of my key passions into my life in the coming month?

The next 3 months?

The next 6 months?

By the end of the year?

Patterns or trends I have noticed this past month:

Positive:

Negative:

In the coming month, I plan to continue to:

In the coming month, I plan to avoid or reduce:

Daily Experience Pages

Date_____

Morning Intention: *Today will be all about...*

Today's Triumphs:

Today's Challenges:

Which of my passions did I touch upon today?

Was this combination of passions successful for me? Why or why not?

Date_____

Morning Intention: *Today will be all about...*

Today's Triumphs:

Today's Challenges:

Which of my passions did I touch upon today?

Was this combination of passions successful for me? Why or why not?

Date_____

Morning Intention: *Today will be all about...*

Today's Triumphs:

Today's Challenges:

Which of my passions did I touch upon today?

Was this combination of passions successful for me? Why or why not?

Date_____

Morning Intention: *Today will be all about...*

Today's Triumphs:

Today's Challenges:

Which of my passions did I touch upon today?

Was this combination of passions successful for me? Why or why not?

Date_____

Morning Intention: *Today will be all about...*

Today's Triumphs:

Today's Challenges:

Which of my passions did I touch upon today?

Was this combination of passions successful for me? Why or why not?

Date_____

Morning Intention: *Today will be all about...*

Today's Triumphs:

Today's Challenges:

Which of my passions did I touch upon today?

Was this combination of passions successful for me? Why or why not?

Date_____

Morning Intention: *Today will be all about...*

Today's Triumphs:

Today's Challenges:

Which of my passions did I touch upon today?

Was this combination of passions successful for me? Why or why not?

Weekly Summary

What were my top three areas of focus this week?

What should I continue to focus on in the coming week?

What will be a new area of focus to add to, or change, from the past week?

What were my top three challenges this week?

How can I improve on each challenge moving forward?

Daily Experience Pages

Date_____

Morning Intention: *Today will be all about...*

Today's Triumphs:

Today's Challenges:

Which of my passions did I touch upon today?

Was this combination of passions successful for me? Why or why not?

Date_____

Morning Intention: *Today will be all about...*

Today's Triumphs:

Today's Challenges:

Which of my passions did I touch upon today?

Was this combination of passions successful for me? Why or why not?

Date_____

Morning Intention: *Today will be all about...*

Today's Triumphs:

Today's Challenges:

Which of my passions did I touch upon today?

Was this combination of passions successful for me? Why or why not?

Date_____

Morning Intention: *Today will be all about...*

Today's Triumphs:

Today's Challenges:

Which of my passions did I touch upon today?

Was this combination of passions successful for me? Why or why not?

Date_____

Morning Intention: *Today will be all about...*

Today's Triumphs:

Today's Challenges:

Which of my passions did I touch upon today?

Was this combination of passions successful for me? Why or why not?

Date_____

Morning Intention: *Today will be all about...*

Today's Triumphs:

Today's Challenges:

Which of my passions did I touch upon today?

Was this combination of passions successful for me? Why or why not?

Date_____

Morning Intention: *Today will be all about...*

Today's Triumphs:

Today's Challenges:

Which of my passions did I touch upon today?

Was this combination of passions successful for me? Why or why not?

Weekly Summary

What were my top three areas of focus this week?

What should I continue to focus on in the coming week?

What will be a new area of focus to add to, or change, from the past week?

What were my top three challenges this week?

How can I improve on each challenge moving forward?

Daily Experience Pages

Date_____

Morning Intention: *Today will be all about...*

Today's Triumphs:

Today's Challenges:

Which of my passions did I touch upon today?

Was this combination of passions successful for me? Why or why not?

Date_____

Morning Intention: *Today will be all about...*

Today's Triumphs:

Today's Challenges:

Which of my passions did I touch upon today?

Was this combination of passions successful for me? Why or why not?

Date_____

Morning Intention: *Today will be all about...*

Today's Triumphs:

Today's Challenges:

Which of my passions did I touch upon today?

Was this combination of passions successful for me? Why or why not?

Date_____

Morning Intention: *Today will be all about...*

Today's Triumphs:

Today's Challenges:

Which of my passions did I touch upon today?

Was this combination of passions successful for me? Why or why not?

Date_____

Morning Intention: *Today will be all about...*

Today's Triumphs:

Today's Challenges:

Which of my passions did I touch upon today?

Was this combination of passions successful for me? Why or why not?

Date_____

Morning Intention: *Today will be all about...*

Today's Triumphs:

Today's Challenges:

Which of my passions did I touch upon today?

Was this combination of passions successful for me? Why or why not?

Date_____

Morning Intention: *Today will be all about...*

Today's Triumphs:

Today's Challenges:

Which of my passions did I touch upon today?

Was this combination of passions successful for me? Why or why not?

Weekly Summary

What were my top three areas of focus this week?

What should I continue to focus on in the coming week?

What will be a new area of focus to add to, or change, from the past week?

What were my top three challenges this week?

How can I improve on each challenge moving forward?

Daily Experience Pages

Date_____

Morning Intention: *Today will be all about...*

Today's Triumphs:

Today's Challenges:

Which of my passions did I touch upon today?

Was this combination of passions successful for me? Why or why not?

Date_____

Morning Intention: *Today will be all about...*

Today's Triumphs:

Today's Challenges:

Which of my passions did I touch upon today?

Was this combination of passions successful for me? Why or why not?

Date_____

Morning Intention: *Today will be all about...*

Today's Triumphs:

Today's Challenges:

Which of my passions did I touch upon today?

Was this combination of passions successful for me? Why or why not?

Date_____

Morning Intention: *Today will be all about...*

Today's Triumphs:

Today's Challenges:

Which of my passions did I touch upon today?

Was this combination of passions successful for me? Why or why not?

Date_____

Morning Intention: *Today will be all about…*

Today's Triumphs:

Today's Challenges:

Which of my passions did I touch upon today?

Was this combination of passions successful for me? Why or why not?

Date_____

Morning Intention: *Today will be all about...*

Today's Triumphs:

Today's Challenges:

Which of my passions did I touch upon today?

Was this combination of passions successful for me? Why or why not?

Date_____

Morning Intention: *Today will be all about...*

Today's Triumphs:

Today's Challenges:

Which of my passions did I touch upon today?

Was this combination of passions successful for me? Why or why not?

Weekly Summary

What were my top three areas of focus this week?

What should I continue to focus on in the coming week?

What will be a new area of focus to add to, or change, from the past week?

What were my top three challenges this week?

How can I improve on each challenge moving forward?

Date_____

Morning Intention: *Today will be all about...*

Today's Triumphs:

Today's Challenges:

Which of my passions did I touch upon today?

Was this combination of passions successful for me? Why or why not?

Date_____

Morning Intention: *Today will be all about...*

Today's Triumphs:

Today's Challenges:

Which of my passions did I touch upon today?

Was this combination of passions successful for me? Why or why not?

Date_____

Morning Intention: *Today will be all about...*

Today's Triumphs:

Today's Challenges:

Which of my passions did I touch upon today?

Was this combination of passions successful for me? Why or why not?

Monthly Reflections: Month 6

If I continue along my current path, is it likely I will incorporate all of my key passions into my life in the coming month?

The next 3 months?

The next 6 months?

By the end of the year?

Patterns or trends I have noticed this past month:

Positive:

Negative:

In the coming month, I plan to continue to:

In the coming month, I plan to avoid or reduce:

Daily Experience Pages

Date_____

Morning Intention: *Today will be all about...*

Today's Triumphs:

Today's Challenges:

Which of my passions did I touch upon today?

Was this combination of passions successful for me? Why or why not?

Date_____

Morning Intention: *Today will be all about...*

Today's Triumphs:

Today's Challenges:

Which of my passions did I touch upon today?

Was this combination of passions successful for me? Why or why not?

Date_____

Morning Intention: *Today will be all about...*

Today's Triumphs:

Today's Challenges:

Which of my passions did I touch upon today?

Was this combination of passions successful for me? Why or why not?

Date_____

Morning Intention: *Today will be all about...*

Today's Triumphs:

Today's Challenges:

Which of my passions did I touch upon today?

Was this combination of passions successful for me? Why or why not?

Date_____

Morning Intention: *Today will be all about...*

Today's Triumphs:

Today's Challenges:

Which of my passions did I touch upon today?

Was this combination of passions successful for me? Why or why not?

Date_____

Morning Intention: *Today will be all about...*

Today's Triumphs:

Today's Challenges:

Which of my passions did I touch upon today?

Was this combination of passions successful for me? Why or why not?

Date_____

Morning Intention: *Today will be all about...*

Today's Triumphs:

Today's Challenges:

Which of my passions did I touch upon today?

Was this combination of passions successful for me? Why or why not?

Weekly Summary

What were my top three areas of focus this week?

What should I continue to focus on in the coming week?

What will be a new area of focus to add to, or change, from the past week?

What were my top three challenges this week?

How can I improve on each challenge moving forward?

Daily Experience Pages

Date_____

Morning Intention: *Today will be all about...*

Today's Triumphs:

Today's Challenges:

Which of my passions did I touch upon today?

Was this combination of passions successful for me? Why or why not?

Date_____

Morning Intention: *Today will be all about…*

Today's Triumphs:

Today's Challenges:

Which of my passions did I touch upon today?

Was this combination of passions successful for me? Why or why not?

Date_____

Morning Intention: *Today will be all about...*

Today's Triumphs:

Today's Challenges:

Which of my passions did I touch upon today?

Was this combination of passions successful for me? Why or why not?

Date_____

Morning Intention: *Today will be all about...*

Today's Triumphs:

Today's Challenges:

Which of my passions did I touch upon today?

Was this combination of passions successful for me? Why or why not?

Date_____

Morning Intention: *Today will be all about...*

Today's Triumphs:

Today's Challenges:

Which of my passions did I touch upon today?

Was this combination of passions successful for me? Why or why not?

Date_____

Morning Intention: *Today will be all about…*

Today's Triumphs:

Today's Challenges:

Which of my passions did I touch upon today?

Was this combination of passions successful for me? Why or why not?

Date_____

Morning Intention: *Today will be all about...*

Today's Triumphs:

Today's Challenges:

Which of my passions did I touch upon today?

Was this combination of passions successful for me? Why or why not?

Weekly Summary

What were my top three areas of focus this week?

What should I continue to focus on in the coming week?

What will be a new area of focus to add to, or change, from the past week?

What were my top three challenges this week?

How can I improve on each challenge moving forward?

Daily Experience Pages

Date_____

Morning Intention: *Today will be all about...*

Today's Triumphs:

Today's Challenges:

Which of my passions did I touch upon today?

Was this combination of passions successful for me? Why or why not?

Date_____

Morning Intention: *Today will be all about...*

Today's Triumphs:

Today's Challenges:

Which of my passions did I touch upon today?

Was this combination of passions successful for me? Why or why not?

Date_____

Morning Intention: *Today will be all about...*

Today's Triumphs:

Today's Challenges:

Which of my passions did I touch upon today?

Was this combination of passions successful for me? Why or why not?

Date_____

Morning Intention: *Today will be all about...*

Today's Triumphs:

Today's Challenges:

Which of my passions did I touch upon today?

Was this combination of passions successful for me? Why or why not?

Date_____

Morning Intention: *Today will be all about...*

Today's Triumphs:

Today's Challenges:

Which of my passions did I touch upon today?

Was this combination of passions successful for me? Why or why not?

Date_____

Morning Intention: *Today will be all about...*

Today's Triumphs:

Today's Challenges:

Which of my passions did I touch upon today?

Was this combination of passions successful for me? Why or why not?

Date_____

Morning Intention: *Today will be all about...*

Today's Triumphs:

Today's Challenges:

Which of my passions did I touch upon today?

Was this combination of passions successful for me? Why or why not?

Weekly Summary

What were my top three areas of focus this week?

What should I continue to focus on in the coming week?

What will be a new area of focus to add to, or change, from the past week?

What were my top three challenges this week?

How can I improve on each challenge moving forward?

Daily Experience Pages

Date_____

Morning Intention: *Today will be all about...*

Today's Triumphs:

Today's Challenges:

Which of my passions did I touch upon today?

Was this combination of passions successful for me? Why or why not?

Date_____

Morning Intention: *Today will be all about...*

Today's Triumphs:

Today's Challenges:

Which of my passions did I touch upon today?

Was this combination of passions successful for me? Why or why not?

Date_____

Morning Intention: *Today will be all about...*

Today's Triumphs:

Today's Challenges:

Which of my passions did I touch upon today?

Was this combination of passions successful for me? Why or why not?

Date_____

Morning Intention: *Today will be all about...*

Today's Triumphs:

Today's Challenges:

Which of my passions did I touch upon today?

Was this combination of passions successful for me? Why or why not?

Date_____

Morning Intention: *Today will be all about...*

Today's Triumphs:

Today's Challenges:

Which of my passions did I touch upon today?

Was this combination of passions successful for me? Why or why not?

Date_____

Morning Intention: *Today will be all about...*

Today's Triumphs:

Today's Challenges:

Which of my passions did I touch upon today?

Was this combination of passions successful for me? Why or why not?

Date_____

Morning Intention: *Today will be all about...*

Today's Triumphs:

Today's Challenges:

Which of my passions did I touch upon today?

Was this combination of passions successful for me? Why or why not?

Weekly Summary

What were my top three areas of focus this week?

What should I continue to focus on in the coming week?

What will be a new area of focus to add to, or change, from the past week?

What were my top three challenges this week?

How can I improve on each challenge moving forward?

Date_____

Morning Intention: *Today will be all about...*

Today's Triumphs:

Today's Challenges:

Which of my passions did I touch upon today?

Was this combination of passions successful for me? Why or why not?

Date_____

Morning Intention: *Today will be all about...*

Today's Triumphs:

Today's Challenges:

Which of my passions did I touch upon today?

Was this combination of passions successful for me? Why or why not?

Date_____

Morning Intention: *Today will be all about...*

Today's Triumphs:

Today's Challenges:

Which of my passions did I touch upon today?

Was this combination of passions successful for me? Why or why not?

Monthly Reflections: Month 7

If I continue along my current path, is it likely I will incorporate all of my key passions into my life in the coming month?

The next 3 months?

The next 6 months?

By the end of the year?

Patterns or trends I have noticed this past month:

Positive:

Negative:

In the coming month, I plan to continue to:

In the coming month, I plan to avoid or reduce:

Daily Experience Pages

Date_____

Morning Intention: *Today will be all about...*

Today's Triumphs:

Today's Challenges:

Which of my passions did I touch upon today?

Was this combination of passions successful for me? Why or why not?

Date_____

Morning Intention: *Today will be all about...*

Today's Triumphs:

Today's Challenges:

Which of my passions did I touch upon today?

Was this combination of passions successful for me? Why or why not?

Date_____

Morning Intention: *Today will be all about...*

Today's Triumphs:

Today's Challenges:

Which of my passions did I touch upon today?

Was this combination of passions successful for me? Why or why not?

Date_____

Morning Intention: *Today will be all about...*

Today's Triumphs:

Today's Challenges:

Which of my passions did I touch upon today?

Was this combination of passions successful for me? Why or why not?

Date_____

Morning Intention: *Today will be all about...*

Today's Triumphs:

Today's Challenges:

Which of my passions did I touch upon today?

Was this combination of passions successful for me? Why or why not?

Date_____

Morning Intention: *Today will be all about...*

Today's Triumphs:

Today's Challenges:

Which of my passions did I touch upon today?

Was this combination of passions successful for me? Why or why not?

Date_____

Morning Intention: *Today will be all about...*

Today's Triumphs:

Today's Challenges:

Which of my passions did I touch upon today?

Was this combination of passions successful for me? Why or why not?

Weekly Summary

What were my top three areas of focus this week?

What should I continue to focus on in the coming week?

What will be a new area of focus to add to, or change, from the past week?

What were my top three challenges this week?

How can I improve on each challenge moving forward?

Daily Experience Pages

Date_____

Morning Intention: *Today will be all about...*

Today's Triumphs:

Today's Challenges:

Which of my passions did I touch upon today?

Was this combination of passions successful for me? Why or why not?

Date_____

Morning Intention: *Today will be all about...*

Today's Triumphs:

Today's Challenges:

Which of my passions did I touch upon today?

Was this combination of passions successful for me? Why or why not?

Date_____

Morning Intention: *Today will be all about...*

Today's Triumphs:

Today's Challenges:

Which of my passions did I touch upon today?

Was this combination of passions successful for me? Why or why not?

Date_____

Morning Intention: *Today will be all about...*

Today's Triumphs:

Today's Challenges:

Which of my passions did I touch upon today?

Was this combination of passions successful for me? Why or why not?

Date_____

Morning Intention: *Today will be all about...*

Today's Triumphs:

Today's Challenges:

Which of my passions did I touch upon today?

Was this combination of passions successful for me? Why or why not?

Date_____

Morning Intention: *Today will be all about...*

Today's Triumphs:

Today's Challenges:

Which of my passions did I touch upon today?

Was this combination of passions successful for me? Why or why not?

Date_____

Morning Intention: *Today will be all about...*

Today's Triumphs:

Today's Challenges:

Which of my passions did I touch upon today?

Was this combination of passions successful for me? Why or why not?

Weekly Summary

What were my top three areas of focus this week?

What should I continue to focus on in the coming week?

What will be a new area of focus to add to, or change, from the past week?

What were my top three challenges this week?

How can I improve on each challenge moving forward?

Daily Experience Pages

Date_____

Morning Intention: *Today will be all about...*

Today's Triumphs:

Today's Challenges:

Which of my passions did I touch upon today?

Was this combination of passions successful for me? Why or why not?

Date_____

Morning Intention: *Today will be all about...*

Today's Triumphs:

Today's Challenges:

Which of my passions did I touch upon today?

Was this combination of passions successful for me? Why or why not?

Date_____

Morning Intention: *Today will be all about...*

Today's Triumphs:

Today's Challenges:

Which of my passions did I touch upon today?

Was this combination of passions successful for me? Why or why not?

Date_____

Morning Intention: *Today will be all about...*

Today's Triumphs:

Today's Challenges:

Which of my passions did I touch upon today?

Was this combination of passions successful for me? Why or why not?

Date_____

Morning Intention: *Today will be all about...*

Today's Triumphs:

Today's Challenges:

Which of my passions did I touch upon today?

Was this combination of passions successful for me? Why or why not?

Date_____

Morning Intention: *Today will be all about...*

Today's Triumphs:

Today's Challenges:

Which of my passions did I touch upon today?

Was this combination of passions successful for me? Why or why not?

Date_____

Morning Intention: *Today will be all about...*

Today's Triumphs:

Today's Challenges:

Which of my passions did I touch upon today?

Was this combination of passions successful for me? Why or why not?

Weekly Summary

What were my top three areas of focus this week?

What should I continue to focus on in the coming week?

What will be a new area of focus to add to, or change, from the past week?

What were my top three challenges this week?

How can I improve on each challenge moving forward?

Daily Experience Pages

Date_____

Morning Intention: *Today will be all about...*

Today's Triumphs:

Today's Challenges:

Which of my passions did I touch upon today?

Was this combination of passions successful for me? Why or why not?

Date_____

Morning Intention: *Today will be all about...*

Today's Triumphs:

Today's Challenges:

Which of my passions did I touch upon today?

Was this combination of passions successful for me? Why or why not?

Date_____

Morning Intention: *Today will be all about...*

Today's Triumphs:

Today's Challenges:

Which of my passions did I touch upon today?

Was this combination of passions successful for me? Why or why not?

Date_____

Morning Intention: *Today will be all about...*

Today's Triumphs:

Today's Challenges:

Which of my passions did I touch upon today?

Was this combination of passions successful for me? Why or why not?

Date_____

Morning Intention: *Today will be all about...*

Today's Triumphs:

Today's Challenges:

Which of my passions did I touch upon today?

Was this combination of passions successful for me? Why or why not?

Date_____

Morning Intention: *Today will be all about...*

Today's Triumphs:

Today's Challenges:

Which of my passions did I touch upon today?

Was this combination of passions successful for me? Why or why not?

Date_____

Morning Intention: *Today will be all about...*

Today's Triumphs:

Today's Challenges:

Which of my passions did I touch upon today?

Was this combination of passions successful for me? Why or why not?

Weekly Summary

What were my top three areas of focus this week?

What should I continue to focus on in the coming week?

What will be a new area of focus to add to, or change, from the past week?

What were my top three challenges this week?

How can I improve on each challenge moving forward?

Date_____

Morning Intention: *Today will be all about...*

Today's Triumphs:

Today's Challenges:

Which of my passions did I touch upon today?

Was this combination of passions successful for me? Why or why not?

Date_____

Morning Intention: *Today will be all about...*

Today's Triumphs:

Today's Challenges:

Which of my passions did I touch upon today?

Was this combination of passions successful for me? Why or why not?

Date_____

Morning Intention: *Today will be all about...*

Today's Triumphs:

Today's Challenges:

Which of my passions did I touch upon today?

Was this combination of passions successful for me? Why or why not?

Monthly Reflections: Month 8

If I continue along my current path, is it likely I will incorporate all of my key passions into my life in the coming month?

The next 3 months?

The next 6 months?

By the end of the year?

Patterns or trends I have noticed this past month:

Positive:

Negative:

In the coming month, I plan to continue to:

In the coming month, I plan to avoid or reduce:

Daily Experience Pages

Date_____

Morning Intention: *Today will be all about...*

Today's Triumphs:

Today's Challenges:

Which of my passions did I touch upon today?

Was this combination of passions successful for me? Why or why not?

Date_____

Morning Intention: *Today will be all about...*

Today's Triumphs:

Today's Challenges:

Which of my passions did I touch upon today?

Was this combination of passions successful for me? Why or why not?

Date_____

Morning Intention: *Today will be all about...*

Today's Triumphs:

Today's Challenges:

Which of my passions did I touch upon today?

Was this combination of passions successful for me? Why or why not?

Date_____

Morning Intention: *Today will be all about...*

Today's Triumphs:

Today's Challenges:

Which of my passions did I touch upon today?

Was this combination of passions successful for me? Why or why not?

Date_____

Morning Intention: *Today will be all about...*

Today's Triumphs:

Today's Challenges:

Which of my passions did I touch upon today?

Was this combination of passions successful for me? Why or why not?

Date_____

Morning Intention: *Today will be all about...*

Today's Triumphs:

Today's Challenges:

Which of my passions did I touch upon today?

Was this combination of passions successful for me? Why or why not?

Date_____

Morning Intention: *Today will be all about...*

Today's Triumphs:

Today's Challenges:

Which of my passions did I touch upon today?

Was this combination of passions successful for me? Why or why not?

Weekly Summary

What were my top three areas of focus this week?

What should I continue to focus on in the coming week?

What will be a new area of focus to add to, or change, from the past week?

What were my top three challenges this week?

How can I improve on each challenge moving forward?

Daily Experience Pages

Date_____

Morning Intention: *Today will be all about...*

Today's Triumphs:

Today's Challenges:

Which of my passions did I touch upon today?

Was this combination of passions successful for me? Why or why not?

Date_____

Morning Intention: *Today will be all about...*

Today's Triumphs:

Today's Challenges:

Which of my passions did I touch upon today?

Was this combination of passions successful for me? Why or why not?

Date_____

Morning Intention: *Today will be all about...*

Today's Triumphs:

Today's Challenges:

Which of my passions did I touch upon today?

Was this combination of passions successful for me? Why or why not?

Date_____

Morning Intention: *Today will be all about…*

Today's Triumphs:

Today's Challenges:

Which of my passions did I touch upon today?

Was this combination of passions successful for me? Why or why not?

Date_____

Morning Intention: *Today will be all about...*

Today's Triumphs:

Today's Challenges:

Which of my passions did I touch upon today?

Was this combination of passions successful for me? Why or why not?

Date_____

Morning Intention: *Today will be all about...*

Today's Triumphs:

Today's Challenges:

Which of my passions did I touch upon today?

Was this combination of passions successful for me? Why or why not?

Date_____

Morning Intention: *Today will be all about...*

Today's Triumphs:

Today's Challenges:

Which of my passions did I touch upon today?

Was this combination of passions successful for me? Why or why not?

Weekly Summary

What were my top three areas of focus this week?

What should I continue to focus on in the coming week?

What will be a new area of focus to add to, or change, from the past week?

What were my top three challenges this week?

How can I improve on each challenge moving forward?

Daily Experience Pages

Date_____

Morning Intention: *Today will be all about...*

Today's Triumphs:

Today's Challenges:

Which of my passions did I touch upon today?

Was this combination of passions successful for me? Why or why not?

Date_____

Morning Intention: *Today will be all about...*

Today's Triumphs:

Today's Challenges:

Which of my passions did I touch upon today?

Was this combination of passions successful for me? Why or why not?

Date_____

Morning Intention: *Today will be all about...*

Today's Triumphs:

Today's Challenges:

Which of my passions did I touch upon today?

Was this combination of passions successful for me? Why or why not?

Date_____

Morning Intention: *Today will be all about...*

Today's Triumphs:

Today's Challenges:

Which of my passions did I touch upon today?

Was this combination of passions successful for me? Why or why not?

Date_____

Morning Intention: *Today will be all about...*

Today's Triumphs:

Today's Challenges:

Which of my passions did I touch upon today?

Was this combination of passions successful for me? Why or why not?

Date_____

Morning Intention: *Today will be all about...*

Today's Triumphs:

Today's Challenges:

Which of my passions did I touch upon today?

Was this combination of passions successful for me? Why or why not?

Date_____

Morning Intention: *Today will be all about...*

Today's Triumphs:

Today's Challenges:

Which of my passions did I touch upon today?

Was this combination of passions successful for me? Why or why not?

Weekly Summary

What were my top three areas of focus this week?

What should I continue to focus on in the coming week?

What will be a new area of focus to add to, or change, from the past week?

What were my top three challenges this week?

How can I improve on each challenge moving forward?

Daily Experience Pages

Date_____

Morning Intention: *Today will be all about...*

Today's Triumphs:

Today's Challenges:

Which of my passions did I touch upon today?

Was this combination of passions successful for me? Why or why not?

Date_____

Morning Intention: *Today will be all about...*

Today's Triumphs:

Today's Challenges:

Which of my passions did I touch upon today?

Was this combination of passions successful for me? Why or why not?

Date_____

Morning Intention: *Today will be all about...*

Today's Triumphs:

Today's Challenges:

Which of my passions did I touch upon today?

Was this combination of passions successful for me? Why or why not?

Date_____

Morning Intention: *Today will be all about...*

Today's Triumphs:

Today's Challenges:

Which of my passions did I touch upon today?

Was this combination of passions successful for me? Why or why not?

Date_____

Morning Intention: *Today will be all about...*

Today's Triumphs:

Today's Challenges:

Which of my passions did I touch upon today?

Was this combination of passions successful for me? Why or why not?

Date_____

Morning Intention: *Today will be all about…*

Today's Triumphs:

Today's Challenges:

Which of my passions did I touch upon today?

Was this combination of passions successful for me? Why or why not?

Date_____

Morning Intention: *Today will be all about...*

Today's Triumphs:

Today's Challenges:

Which of my passions did I touch upon today?

Was this combination of passions successful for me? Why or why not?

Weekly Summary

What were my top three areas of focus this week?

What should I continue to focus on in the coming week?

What will be a new area of focus to add to, or change, from the past week?

What were my top three challenges this week?

How can I improve on each challenge moving forward?

Date_____

Morning Intention: *Today will be all about...*

Today's Triumphs:

Today's Challenges:

Which of my passions did I touch upon today?

Was this combination of passions successful for me? Why or why not?

Date_____

Morning Intention: *Today will be all about...*

Today's Triumphs:

Today's Challenges:

Which of my passions did I touch upon today?

Was this combination of passions successful for me? Why or why not?

Date_____

Morning Intention: *Today will be all about...*

Today's Triumphs:

Today's Challenges:

Which of my passions did I touch upon today?

Was this combination of passions successful for me? Why or why not?

Monthly Reflections: Month 9

If I continue along my current path, is it likely I will incorporate all of my key passions into my life in the coming month?

The next 3 months?

The next 6 months?

By the end of the year?

Patterns or trends I have noticed this past month:

Positive:

Negative:

In the coming month, I plan to continue to:

In the coming month, I plan to avoid or reduce:

Daily Experience Pages

Date_____

Morning Intention: *Today will be all about...*

Today's Triumphs:

Today's Challenges:

Which of my passions did I touch upon today?

Was this combination of passions successful for me? Why or why not?

Date_____

Morning Intention: *Today will be all about...*

Today's Triumphs:

Today's Challenges:

Which of my passions did I touch upon today?

Was this combination of passions successful for me? Why or why not?

Date_____

Morning Intention: *Today will be all about...*

Today's Triumphs:

Today's Challenges:

Which of my passions did I touch upon today?

Was this combination of passions successful for me? Why or why not?

Date_____

Morning Intention: *Today will be all about...*

Today's Triumphs:

Today's Challenges:

Which of my passions did I touch upon today?

Was this combination of passions successful for me? Why or why not?

Date_____

Morning Intention: *Today will be all about...*

Today's Triumphs:

Today's Challenges:

Which of my passions did I touch upon today?

Was this combination of passions successful for me? Why or why not?

Date_____

Morning Intention: *Today will be all about...*

Today's Triumphs:

Today's Challenges:

Which of my passions did I touch upon today?

Was this combination of passions successful for me? Why or why not?

Date_____

Morning Intention: *Today will be all about...*

Today's Triumphs:

Today's Challenges:

Which of my passions did I touch upon today?

Was this combination of passions successful for me? Why or why not?

Weekly Summary

What were my top three areas of focus this week?

What should I continue to focus on in the coming week?

What will be a new area of focus to add to, or change, from the past week?

What were my top three challenges this week?

How can I improve on each challenge moving forward?

Daily Experience Pages

Date_____

Morning Intention: *Today will be all about...*

Today's Triumphs:

Today's Challenges:

Which of my passions did I touch upon today?

Was this combination of passions successful for me? Why or why not?

Date_____

Morning Intention: *Today will be all about...*

Today's Triumphs:

Today's Challenges:

Which of my passions did I touch upon today?

Was this combination of passions successful for me? Why or why not?

Date_____

Morning Intention: *Today will be all about...*

Today's Triumphs:

Today's Challenges:

Which of my passions did I touch upon today?

Was this combination of passions successful for me? Why or why not?

Date_____

Morning Intention: *Today will be all about...*

Today's Triumphs:

Today's Challenges:

Which of my passions did I touch upon today?

Was this combination of passions successful for me? Why or why not?

Date_____

Morning Intention: *Today will be all about...*

Today's Triumphs:

Today's Challenges:

Which of my passions did I touch upon today?

Was this combination of passions successful for me? Why or why not?

Date_____

Morning Intention: *Today will be all about...*

Today's Triumphs:

Today's Challenges:

Which of my passions did I touch upon today?

Was this combination of passions successful for me? Why or why not?

Date_____

Morning Intention: *Today will be all about...*

Today's Triumphs:

Today's Challenges:

Which of my passions did I touch upon today?

Was this combination of passions successful for me? Why or why not?

Weekly Summary

What were my top three areas of focus this week?

What should I continue to focus on in the coming week?

What will be a new area of focus to add to, or change, from the past week?

What were my top three challenges this week?

How can I improve on each challenge moving forward?

Daily Experience Pages

Date_____

Morning Intention: *Today will be all about...*

Today's Triumphs:

Today's Challenges:

Which of my passions did I touch upon today?

Was this combination of passions successful for me? Why or why not?

Date_____

Morning Intention: *Today will be all about...*

Today's Triumphs:

Today's Challenges:

Which of my passions did I touch upon today?

Was this combination of passions successful for me? Why or why not?

Date_____

Morning Intention: *Today will be all about...*

Today's Triumphs:

Today's Challenges:

Which of my passions did I touch upon today?

Was this combination of passions successful for me? Why or why not?

Date_____

Morning Intention: *Today will be all about...*

Today's Triumphs:

Today's Challenges:

Which of my passions did I touch upon today?

Was this combination of passions successful for me? Why or why not?

Date_____

Morning Intention: *Today will be all about...*

Today's Triumphs:

Today's Challenges:

Which of my passions did I touch upon today?

Was this combination of passions successful for me? Why or why not?

Date_____

Morning Intention: *Today will be all about...*

Today's Triumphs:

Today's Challenges:

Which of my passions did I touch upon today?

Was this combination of passions successful for me? Why or why not?

Date_____

Morning Intention: *Today will be all about...*

Today's Triumphs:

Today's Challenges:

Which of my passions did I touch upon today?

Was this combination of passions successful for me? Why or why not?

Weekly Summary

What were my top three areas of focus this week?

What should I continue to focus on in the coming week?

What will be a new area of focus to add to, or change, from the past week?

What were my top three challenges this week?

How can I improve on each challenge moving forward?

Daily Experience Pages

Date_____

Morning Intention: *Today will be all about...*

Today's Triumphs:

Today's Challenges:

Which of my passions did I touch upon today?

Was this combination of passions successful for me? Why or why not?

Date_____

Morning Intention: *Today will be all about...*

Today's Triumphs:

Today's Challenges:

Which of my passions did I touch upon today?

Was this combination of passions successful for me? Why or why not?

Date_____

Morning Intention: *Today will be all about...*

Today's Triumphs:

Today's Challenges:

Which of my passions did I touch upon today?

Was this combination of passions successful for me? Why or why not?

Date_____

Morning Intention: *Today will be all about...*

Today's Triumphs:

Today's Challenges:

Which of my passions did I touch upon today?

Was this combination of passions successful for me? Why or why not?

Date_____

Morning Intention: *Today will be all about...*

Today's Triumphs:

Today's Challenges:

Which of my passions did I touch upon today?

Was this combination of passions successful for me? Why or why not?

Date_____

Morning Intention: *Today will be all about...*

Today's Triumphs:

Today's Challenges:

Which of my passions did I touch upon today?

Was this combination of passions successful for me? Why or why not?

Date_____

Morning Intention: *Today will be all about...*

Today's Triumphs:

Today's Challenges:

Which of my passions did I touch upon today?

Was this combination of passions successful for me? Why or why not?

Weekly Summary

What were my top three areas of focus this week?

What should I continue to focus on in the coming week?

What will be a new area of focus to add to, or change, from the past week?

What were my top three challenges this week?

How can I improve on each challenge moving forward?

Date_____

Morning Intention: *Today will be all about...*

Today's Triumphs:

Today's Challenges:

Which of my passions did I touch upon today?

Was this combination of passions successful for me? Why or why not?

Date_____

Morning Intention: *Today will be all about...*

Today's Triumphs:

Today's Challenges:

Which of my passions did I touch upon today?

Was this combination of passions successful for me? Why or why not?

Date_____

Morning Intention: *Today will be all about...*

Today's Triumphs:

Today's Challenges:

Which of my passions did I touch upon today?

Was this combination of passions successful for me? Why or why not?

Monthly Reflections: Month 10

If I continue along my current path, is it likely I will incorporate all of my key passions into my life in the coming month?

The next 3 months?

The next 6 months?

By the end of the year?

Patterns or trends I have noticed this past month:

Positive:

Negative:

In the coming month, I plan to continue to:

In the coming month, I plan to avoid or reduce:

Daily Experience Pages

Date_____

Morning Intention: *Today will be all about...*

Today's Triumphs:

Today's Challenges:

Which of my passions did I touch upon today?

Was this combination of passions successful for me? Why or why not?

Date_____

Morning Intention: *Today will be all about...*

Today's Triumphs:

Today's Challenges:

Which of my passions did I touch upon today?

Was this combination of passions successful for me? Why or why not?

Date_____

Morning Intention: *Today will be all about...*

Today's Triumphs:

Today's Challenges:

Which of my passions did I touch upon today?

Was this combination of passions successful for me? Why or why not?

Date_____

Morning Intention: *Today will be all about...*

Today's Triumphs:

Today's Challenges:

Which of my passions did I touch upon today?

Was this combination of passions successful for me? Why or why not?

Date_____

Morning Intention: *Today will be all about...*

Today's Triumphs:

Today's Challenges:

Which of my passions did I touch upon today?

Was this combination of passions successful for me? Why or why not?

Date_____

Morning Intention: *Today will be all about...*

Today's Triumphs:

Today's Challenges:

Which of my passions did I touch upon today?

Was this combination of passions successful for me? Why or why not?

Date_____

Morning Intention: *Today will be all about...*

Today's Triumphs:

Today's Challenges:

Which of my passions did I touch upon today?

Was this combination of passions successful for me? Why or why not?

Weekly Summary

What were my top three areas of focus this week?

What should I continue to focus on in the coming week?

What will be a new area of focus to add to, or change, from the past week?

What were my top three challenges this week?

How can I improve on each challenge moving forward?

Daily Experience Pages

Date_____

Morning Intention: *Today will be all about...*

Today's Triumphs:

Today's Challenges:

Which of my passions did I touch upon today?

Was this combination of passions successful for me? Why or why not?

Date_____

Morning Intention: *Today will be all about...*

Today's Triumphs:

Today's Challenges:

Which of my passions did I touch upon today?

Was this combination of passions successful for me? Why or why not?

Date_____

Morning Intention: *Today will be all about...*

Today's Triumphs:

Today's Challenges:

Which of my passions did I touch upon today?

Was this combination of passions successful for me? Why or why not?

Date_____

Morning Intention: *Today will be all about...*

Today's Triumphs:

Today's Challenges:

Which of my passions did I touch upon today?

Was this combination of passions successful for me? Why or why not?

Date_____

Morning Intention: *Today will be all about...*

Today's Triumphs:

Today's Challenges:

Which of my passions did I touch upon today?

Was this combination of passions successful for me? Why or why not?

Date_____

Morning Intention: *Today will be all about...*

Today's Triumphs:

Today's Challenges:

Which of my passions did I touch upon today?

Was this combination of passions successful for me? Why or why not?

Date_____

Morning Intention: *Today will be all about...*

Today's Triumphs:

Today's Challenges:

Which of my passions did I touch upon today?

Was this combination of passions successful for me? Why or why not?

Weekly Summary

What were my top three areas of focus this week?

What should I continue to focus on in the coming week?

What will be a new area of focus to add to, or change, from the past week?

What were my top three challenges this week?

How can I improve on each challenge moving forward?

Daily Experience Pages

Date_____

Morning Intention: *Today will be all about...*

Today's Triumphs:

Today's Challenges:

Which of my passions did I touch upon today?

Was this combination of passions successful for me? Why or why not?

Date_____

Morning Intention: *Today will be all about...*

Today's Triumphs:

Today's Challenges:

Which of my passions did I touch upon today?

Was this combination of passions successful for me? Why or why not?

Date_____

Morning Intention: *Today will be all about...*

Today's Triumphs:

Today's Challenges:

Which of my passions did I touch upon today?

Was this combination of passions successful for me? Why or why not?

Date_____

Morning Intention: *Today will be all about...*

Today's Triumphs:

Today's Challenges:

Which of my passions did I touch upon today?

Was this combination of passions successful for me? Why or why not?

Date_____

Morning Intention: *Today will be all about...*

Today's Triumphs:

Today's Challenges:

Which of my passions did I touch upon today?

Was this combination of passions successful for me? Why or why not?

Date_____

Morning Intention: *Today will be all about...*

Today's Triumphs:

Today's Challenges:

Which of my passions did I touch upon today?

Was this combination of passions successful for me? Why or why not?

Date_____

Morning Intention: *Today will be all about...*

Today's Triumphs:

Today's Challenges:

Which of my passions did I touch upon today?

Was this combination of passions successful for me? Why or why not?

Weekly Summary

What were my top three areas of focus this week?

What should I continue to focus on in the coming week?

What will be a new area of focus to add to, or change, from the past week?

What were my top three challenges this week?

How can I improve on each challenge moving forward?

Daily Experience Pages

Date_____

Morning Intention: *Today will be all about...*

Today's Triumphs:

Today's Challenges:

Which of my passions did I touch upon today?

Was this combination of passions successful for me? Why or why not?

Date_____

Morning Intention: *Today will be all about...*

Today's Triumphs:

Today's Challenges:

Which of my passions did I touch upon today?

Was this combination of passions successful for me? Why or why not?

Date_____

Morning Intention: *Today will be all about...*

Today's Triumphs:

Today's Challenges:

Which of my passions did I touch upon today?

Was this combination of passions successful for me? Why or why not?

Date_____

Morning Intention: *Today will be all about...*

Today's Triumphs:

Today's Challenges:

Which of my passions did I touch upon today?

Was this combination of passions successful for me? Why or why not?

Date_____

Morning Intention: *Today will be all about...*

Today's Triumphs:

Today's Challenges:

Which of my passions did I touch upon today?

Was this combination of passions successful for me? Why or why not?

Date_____

Morning Intention: *Today will be all about...*

Today's Triumphs:

Today's Challenges:

Which of my passions did I touch upon today?

Was this combination of passions successful for me? Why or why not?

Date_____

Morning Intention: *Today will be all about...*

Today's Triumphs:

Today's Challenges:

Which of my passions did I touch upon today?

Was this combination of passions successful for me? Why or why not?

Weekly Summary

What were my top three areas of focus this week?

What should I continue to focus on in the coming week?

What will be a new area of focus to add to, or change, from the past week?

What were my top three challenges this week?

How can I improve on each challenge moving forward?

Date_____

Morning Intention: *Today will be all about...*

Today's Triumphs:

Today's Challenges:

Which of my passions did I touch upon today?

Was this combination of passions successful for me? Why or why not?

Date_____

Morning Intention: *Today will be all about...*

Today's Triumphs:

Today's Challenges:

Which of my passions did I touch upon today?

Was this combination of passions successful for me? Why or why not?

Date_____

Morning Intention: *Today will be all about...*

Today's Triumphs:

Today's Challenges:

Which of my passions did I touch upon today?

Was this combination of passions successful for me? Why or why not?

Monthly Reflections: Month 11

If I continue along my current path, is it likely I will incorporate all of my key passions into my life in the coming month?

The next 3 months?

The next 6 months?

By the end of the year?

Patterns or trends I have noticed this past month:

Positive:

Negative:

In the coming month, I plan to continue to:

In the coming month, I plan to avoid or reduce:

Daily Experience Pages

Date_____

Morning Intention: *Today will be all about...*

Today's Triumphs:

Today's Challenges:

Which of my passions did I touch upon today?

Was this combination of passions successful for me? Why or why not?

Date_____

Morning Intention: *Today will be all about...*

Today's Triumphs:

Today's Challenges:

Which of my passions did I touch upon today?

Was this combination of passions successful for me? Why or why not?

Date_____

Morning Intention: *Today will be all about...*

Today's Triumphs:

Today's Challenges:

Which of my passions did I touch upon today?

Was this combination of passions successful for me? Why or why not?

Date_____

Morning Intention: *Today will be all about...*

Today's Triumphs:

Today's Challenges:

Which of my passions did I touch upon today?

Was this combination of passions successful for me? Why or why not?

Date_____

Morning Intention: *Today will be all about...*

Today's Triumphs:

Today's Challenges:

Which of my passions did I touch upon today?

Was this combination of passions successful for me? Why or why not?

Date_____

Morning Intention: *Today will be all about...*

Today's Triumphs:

Today's Challenges:

Which of my passions did I touch upon today?

Was this combination of passions successful for me? Why or why not?

Date_____

Morning Intention: *Today will be all about...*

Today's Triumphs:

Today's Challenges:

Which of my passions did I touch upon today?

Was this combination of passions successful for me? Why or why not?

Weekly Summary

What were my top three areas of focus this week?

What should I continue to focus on in the coming week?

What will be a new area of focus to add to, or change, from the past week?

What were my top three challenges this week?

How can I improve on each challenge moving forward?

Daily Experience Pages

Date_____

Morning Intention: *Today will be all about...*

Today's Triumphs:

Today's Challenges:

Which of my passions did I touch upon today?

Was this combination of passions successful for me? Why or why not?

Date_____

Morning Intention: *Today will be all about...*

Today's Triumphs:

Today's Challenges:

Which of my passions did I touch upon today?

Was this combination of passions successful for me? Why or why not?

Date_____

Morning Intention: *Today will be all about...*

Today's Triumphs:

Today's Challenges:

Which of my passions did I touch upon today?

Was this combination of passions successful for me? Why or why not?

Date_____

Morning Intention: *Today will be all about...*

Today's Triumphs:

Today's Challenges:

Which of my passions did I touch upon today?

Was this combination of passions successful for me? Why or why not?

Date_____

Morning Intention: *Today will be all about...*

Today's Triumphs:

Today's Challenges:

Which of my passions did I touch upon today?

Was this combination of passions successful for me? Why or why not?

Date_____

Morning Intention: *Today will be all about...*

Today's Triumphs:

Today's Challenges:

Which of my passions did I touch upon today?

Was this combination of passions successful for me? Why or why not?

Date_____

Morning Intention: *Today will be all about...*

Today's Triumphs:

Today's Challenges:

Which of my passions did I touch upon today?

Was this combination of passions successful for me? Why or why not?

Weekly Summary

What were my top three areas of focus this week?

What should I continue to focus on in the coming week?

What will be a new area of focus to add to, or change, from the past week?

What were my top three challenges this week?

How can I improve on each challenge moving forward?

Daily Experience Pages

Date_____

Morning Intention: *Today will be all about...*

Today's Triumphs:

Today's Challenges:

Which of my passions did I touch upon today?

Was this combination of passions successful for me? Why or why not?

Date_____

Morning Intention: *Today will be all about...*

Today's Triumphs:

Today's Challenges:

Which of my passions did I touch upon today?

Was this combination of passions successful for me? Why or why not?

Date_____

Morning Intention: *Today will be all about...*

Today's Triumphs:

Today's Challenges:

Which of my passions did I touch upon today?

Was this combination of passions successful for me? Why or why not?

Date_____

Morning Intention: *Today will be all about...*

Today's Triumphs:

Today's Challenges:

Which of my passions did I touch upon today?

Was this combination of passions successful for me? Why or why not?

Date_____

Morning Intention: *Today will be all about...*

Today's Triumphs:

Today's Challenges:

Which of my passions did I touch upon today?

Was this combination of passions successful for me? Why or why not?

Date_____

Morning Intention: *Today will be all about...*

Today's Triumphs:

Today's Challenges:

Which of my passions did I touch upon today?

Was this combination of passions successful for me? Why or why not?

Date_____

Morning Intention: *Today will be all about...*

Today's Triumphs:

Today's Challenges:

Which of my passions did I touch upon today?

Was this combination of passions successful for me? Why or why not?

Weekly Summary

What were my top three areas of focus this week?

What should I continue to focus on in the coming week?

What will be a new area of focus to add to, or change, from the past week?

What were my top three challenges this week?

How can I improve on each challenge moving forward?

Daily Experience Pages

Date_____

Morning Intention: *Today will be all about...*

Today's Triumphs:

Today's Challenges:

Which of my passions did I touch upon today?

Was this combination of passions successful for me? Why or why not?

Date_____

Morning Intention: *Today will be all about...*

Today's Triumphs:

Today's Challenges:

Which of my passions did I touch upon today?

Was this combination of passions successful for me? Why or why not?

Date_____

Morning Intention: *Today will be all about...*

Today's Triumphs:

Today's Challenges:

Which of my passions did I touch upon today?

Was this combination of passions successful for me? Why or why not?

Date_____

Morning Intention: *Today will be all about...*

Today's Triumphs:

Today's Challenges:

Which of my passions did I touch upon today?

Was this combination of passions successful for me? Why or why not?

Date_____

Morning Intention: *Today will be all about...*

Today's Triumphs:

Today's Challenges:

Which of my passions did I touch upon today?

Was this combination of passions successful for me? Why or why not?

Date_____

Morning Intention: *Today will be all about...*

Today's Triumphs:

Today's Challenges:

Which of my passions did I touch upon today?

Was this combination of passions successful for me? Why or why not?

Date_____

Morning Intention: *Today will be all about...*

Today's Triumphs:

Today's Challenges:

Which of my passions did I touch upon today?

Was this combination of passions successful for me? Why or why not?

Weekly Summary

What were my top three areas of focus this week?

What should I continue to focus on in the coming week?

What will be a new area of focus to add to, or change, from the past week?

What were my top three challenges this week?

How can I improve on each challenge moving forward?

Date_____

Morning Intention: *Today will be all about...*

Today's Triumphs:

Today's Challenges:

Which of my passions did I touch upon today?

Was this combination of passions successful for me? Why or why not?

Date_____

Morning Intention: *Today will be all about...*

Today's Triumphs:

Today's Challenges:

Which of my passions did I touch upon today?

Was this combination of passions successful for me? Why or why not?

Date_____

Morning Intention: *Today will be all about...*

Today's Triumphs:

Today's Challenges:

Which of my passions did I touch upon today?

Was this combination of passions successful for me? Why or why not?

Monthly Reflections: Month 12

If I continue along my current path, is it likely I will incorporate all of my key passions into my life in the coming month?

The next 3 months?

The next 6 months?

By the end of the year?

Patterns or trends I have noticed this past month:

Positive:

Negative:

In the coming month, I plan to continue to:

In the coming month, I plan to avoid or reduce:

Year in Review

Congratulations! You have taken this past year into your hands, and have lived with intention, purpose, and reflective insights. This is more than many people do, and while it's not about comparing ourselves to others, know that you have given yourself a gift that will continue to open up and blossom. As you continue to get to know your authentic self, your true passions, and (equally as important) how to manage these in daily compartments, over time you will find a peaceful sense of balance and focus amid the wide variety in your life.

Now set aside a quiet session in a comfortable place. If you enjoy listening to music, cue it up. Make some tea. Or go to a favorite spot in nature. Whatever makes you comfortable, prepare to reflect on the past year, and slowly turn your thoughts to the coming year.

First, re-read your entries from the past year. You may find it interesting to open the journal to random pages and see what messages emerge. Or, you may appreciate your sequential developments, and read your journal in chronological order—the book of you. Remember to also revisit your Weekly Summary pages, and your Monthly Reflections. Are you spotting any trends?

Finally, ask yourself these questions. You do not need to write them down right away. Think, mull, ponder, and reflect over them.

Dates of journal use, from_____to_____

How would I describe the past year?

Am I living the life I envisioned, incorporating most of my key passions?

What changes have I experienced?

How have I evolved in the past year?

What would I still like to improve upon?

Are there any new passions that have emerged for me in the past year?

What would I like to explore further?

What goals can I set for the coming year?

Set my intention for the coming year: *The year ahead will be all about...*

About the Author

Gilat Ben-Dor, MBA, CSW is a speaker, author, and the founder of GUSTO POWER®, a personal and professional development program that helps Multi-Passionate Professionals™ successfully manage their many talents. A creative "multipreneur" herself, Gilat has created several successful businesses, including a wine academy, a publishing company, and an online emporium featuring Gilat's art and photography. Gilat is also an adjunct faculty member at a nationally recognized university. She holds an MBA in Global Management and lives in Scottsdale, Arizona.

For more information about Gilat Ben-Dor, visit her central web site,
GilatBen-Dor.com

To learn more about Gilat Ben-Dor's GUSTO POWER® success strategy program for Multi-Passionate Professionals™, visit **GustoPower.com**

For *The Rainbow Blueprint Action Journal's* official website,
visit **RainbowBlueprint.com**

Rainbow Blueprint Opportunities

Speaking, Coaching, Consulting and Workshops with Gilat Ben-Dor

Although your experiences working with *The Rainbow Blueprint Action Journal* may have been private and intense, your new discoveries may benefit your organization, including how you can manage multiple passions and projects through planning and action. Imagine sharing your insights and inspirations from *The Rainbow Blueprint Action Journal* with your company and your network.

Dynamic speaker, author, coach and consultant Gilat Ben-Dor is passionate about bringing more creativity, productivity, and peace of mind to Multi-Passionate Professionals™ and their teams.

For more information about booking Gilat Ben-Dor for your organization, please email **info@GustoPower.com**

Gilat Ben-Dor's presentation formats include keynote speeches, break-out sessions, workshops/seminars, webinars, consulting, and Platinum one-on-one coaching.

Suggested participants include:

- Leaders & Managers
- Creative Professionals
- Associations
- Entrepreneurs
- Universities

As a complement to the message of her book, *The Rainbow Blueprint: An Action Journal for Those with Many Passions*, Gilat Ben-Dor offers a special presentation:

Your Rainbow Blueprint: A Prism of Clarity™
Filled with opportunities for group participation and personal reflection, this self-discovery presentation can be presented both as a workshop or a traditional keynote speech. Both business and personal-growth groups can benefit from this message about finding stillness, focus, and renewed purpose through this pairing of live engagement and versatile tools. (Also recommended for groups in transition or healing.)

Additional presentation topics by Gilat Ben-Dor include:

GUSTO POWER®: Power Skills for the Multi-Passionate Professional™
Gilat's signature keynote of the Gusto Power® program, this presentation is ideal for both corporate and entrepreneurial groups. Through engaging stories, humor and pertinent case studies, the audience will take away a new understanding of the benefits of exploring our diverse sets of talents. Participants will learn simple, effective "Power Skills" they can apply immediately to increase personal satisfaction, workplace morale, and professional productivity.

Like a Diamond: The Brilliance and Benefits of Multi-Faceted Careers™
Many of us have been conditioned to believe that professionally, we must only do one thing and be one thing. But this shoe does not fit everyone, and holding back can short-change both ourselves and our organizations. This eye-opening presentation will reveal the untapped potential — and how to unleash it

— from each individual, and how this immense pool of hidden talents can result in profitable partnerships and synergies.

Creative Nine-to-Five: Branching Out While Punching In™

Although specialists have traditionally been valued, the definition of a valued employee is rapidly changing. With economic shakedowns and a new corporate landscape, today's MVE (Most Valuable Employee) can do more by calling upon all sides of themselves. This keynote combines case studies, personal experiences, and an uplifting message that celebrates the value employees offer their organization by being multi-faceted professionals.

> **To obtain a free report, "The Top 5 Mistakes Multi-Passionate Professionals Make," visit http://GustoPower.com**

Book and journal discounts available for bulk purchases. For details, please inquire with the publisher: info@GilatMedia.com

www.ingramcontent.com/pod-product-compliance
Lightning Source LLC
Chambersburg PA
CBHW080527170426
43195CB00016B/2493